Congo
the Painter

by Josephine Parks

Harcourt
SCHOOL PUBLISHERS

Cover ©Getty Images; 2 ©AAP; 3 ©Robert Maier/Animals Animals; 4 ©Patti Murry/Animals Animals; 5 ©Alamy Images; 6–8 ©Getty Images.

Printed in China

ISBN 10: 0-15-351302-0
ISBN 13: 978-0-15-351302-2

Ordering Options
ISBN 10: 0-15-351211-3 (Grade 1 Advanced Collection)
ISBN 13: 978-0-15-351211-7 (Grade 1 Advanced Collection)
ISBN 10: 0-15-358030-5 (package of 5)
ISBN 13: 978-0-15-358030-7 (package of 5)

3 4 5 6 7 8 9 10   468   15 14 13 12 11 10 09 08

Look at this art. Do you like the paintings? Do you know who did both of these paintings?

People didn't do the paintings. An animal did the paintings!

A hamster did not paint the paintings. A hamster can't paint. A hamster can run on a wheel, but it can't hold a brush!

A duck did not do the paintings.
A duck can't paint. A duck can quack
and waddle, but it can't hold a brush!

A cat did not do the paintings.
A cat can't paint. A cat can jump from
here to there, but it can't hold a brush!

Can you guess what animal did the paintings? It was this chimpanzee! His name was Congo.

Congo was very good at painting. He liked to put lots of colors of paint on his paper. He could carry a paintbrush in his hand to make his artwork.

Congo with one of his paintings

Congo lived and painted until 1964. Some people still like to buy Congo's paintings. People pay a great deal of money for them. In 2005, a man bought two of Congo's paintings for $25,000!

Would you like to buy one of Congo's other paintings? Which one of Congo's paintings would you like to have?